INFORMATION
EXPLORER
JUNIOR

Mind Your Manners Online

by Phyllis Cornwall

CHERRY LAKE PUBLISHING · ANN ARBOR, MICHIGAN

4/12

A NOTE TO PARENTS AND TEACHERS: Please remind your children how to stay safe online before they do the activities in this book.

CHERRY
LAKE
Publishing

A NOTE TO KIDS: Always remember your safety comes first!

Published in the United States of America
by Cherry Lake Publishing
Ann Arbor, Michigan
www.cherrylakepublishing.com

Content Adviser: Gail Dickinson, PhD, Associate Professor, Old Dominion University

Book design and illustration: The Design Lab

Photo credits: Cover and pages 9 and 16, ©Dmitriy Shironosov/Shutterstock, Inc.; page 5, ©Monkey Business Images/Shutterstock, Inc.; page 6, ©Fotokostic/Shutterstock, Inc.; page 10, ©Tyler Olson/Shutterstock, Inc.; page 11, ©Ilike/Shutterstock, Inc.; page 13, ©Rob Marmion/Shutterstock, Inc.; page 15, ©Golden Pixels LLC/Shutterstock, Inc.; page 19, ©iStockphoto.com/Imagesbybarbara; page 20, ©iStockphoto.com/zorani

Library of Congress Cataloging-in-Publication Data

Cornwall, Phyllis.
  Mind your manners online / by Phyllis Cornwall.
    p. cm.—(Information explorer junior)
  Includes bibliographical references and index.
  ISBN 978-1-61080-363-2 (lib. bdg.)—ISBN 978-1-61080-372-4 (e-book)—
ISBN 978-1-61080-388-5 (pbk.)
  1. Online etiquette—Juvenile literature. I. Title.
  TK5105.878.C66 2012
  395.5—dc23   2011034506

Cherry Lake Publishing would like to acknowledge
the work of The Partnership for 21st Century Skills.
Please visit www.21stcenturyskills.org for more information.

Printed in the United States of America
Corporate Graphics Inc.
January 2012
CLSP10

Table of Contents

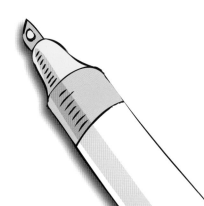

CHAPTER ONE

Minding Your Manners Online

Have you heard people say the word **"etiquette"** (EH-ti-kut)? They are talking about good manners.

Wiping messes on your sleeve is bad etiquette.

Etiquette is using good and polite behavior. Sometimes rules are being followed. But etiquette is more than rules. Good table manners are part of etiquette. Do you slurp your drink? Do you wipe your messy mouth on your sleeve? That's not good etiquette.

Putting trash where it belongs is part of good etiquette.

You aren't breaking any rules. But people will think you are not very polite.

Do you throw trash on the floor? That is not good etiquette, either. Schools have rules about cleaning up trash.

So sometimes there are manners. And sometimes there are rules. Both are part of etiquette. Using etiquette shows you are respectful of others.

To get a copy of this activity, visit
www.cherrylakepublishing.com/activities.

Activity

Is etiquette the same everywhere? Draw a line
down the middle of a piece of paper. You now
have two columns. At the top of one column, write
"My House." Label the other column "A Friend's
House." List five things that are considered good
manners under each location. Are some manners
the same? Are some different? Why is that so?

Being a good sport is part of good etiquette
when you play a game.

Using etiquette **online** is important, too. Online etiquette is showing respect for others. It makes using the Internet safer and more fun.

To get a copy of this activity, visit www.cherrylakepublishing.com/activities.

Activity

On a new peice of paper, write "Online Etiquette." List five things you think are good online manners. Compare this list to the lists from the last activity. Which manners are the same? Which are different?

Always respect others online!

CHAPTER TWO

Online Etiquette: Your Words

Having **privacy** means wanting to keep something to yourself. You may not want to share your thoughts or words. You don't want other people to hear them.

I hope none of my friends saw me fall in the cafeteria today.

Anyone can read your thoughts if you write them down.

Thinking about something is always private. No one knows what you are thinking. But words can be written on a piece of paper. That might not be private. Say you gave a friend a note, and she loses it. Your note might be found. Someone else might read it. Your note had been private. Now it is not.

Most things on the Internet are public.

The same thing can happen online. You might **post** words online. Your words might be seen by many people. They might be copied. They could be sent to people you don't even know. You may think places online are private. But writing on the Internet is public. You might have shared your words with people you trust. Your words can still become public.

Suppose you sent a picture to a friend online. The picture shows you doing something silly. Your friend thinks the picture is very funny. He sends it to other people. But you didn't say he could do that. Now other people can see the photo. It might embarrass you. It might even cause you to get into trouble.

You never know who might see the things you post online.

Always ask yourself these questions before posting something online:

1. Would I say this to my friend out loud?
2. Could someone print what I wrote and show it to her parents?
3. Would my parents or teacher like my words?
4. How Might the person reading this feel?

Always think before you post!

To get a copy of this activity, visit www.cherrylakepublishing.com/activities.

Activity

What is the difference between public and private? Below is a list of places and things. Can you tell which are public and which are private?

1. The library
2. A neighbor's yard
3. A newspaper
4. Your journal

Be careful to avoid posting anything that could hurt someone or get you in trouble.

Answers: 1. public, 2. private, 3. public, 4. private

CHAPTER THREE

Online Etiquette: Blogging

Following someone's **blog** can be fun. You can learn a lot. Blogs are like online diaries or journals. The writer posts his or her thoughts. They might be about events, places, or people. Most blogs let visitors leave comments. Practice good online etiquette when you're visiting a blog.

Do you want to post a comment on a blog? Here's a good rule to follow. Can't think of anything nice to say? Then don't say anything at all. You don't have to agree with everything you read. But there is

Be friendly to people online just like you would if you met them in person.

always a respectful way to say something. Your comments should never be rude or hurtful. Let's say you went to someone's home. Would you say bad things about the furniture there? Visiting a blog is like being a guest in someone's home. Treat the writer and his guests with respect.

What if you make a mistake? You might post the same comment more than once.

Apologize to the blog writer by e-mail. You could also post your apology with another comment.

Things you read on a blog might make you angry. They might upset you. Stop visiting that blog. Don't waste your time posting comments. Move on and find a new blog. There are so many fun blogs on the Internet. You'll easily find a better one.

There is always another fun new blog to read online.

To get a copy of this activity, visit www.cherrylakepublishing.com/activities.

Activity

Suppose you had your own blog. You want your visitors to follow good etiquette. Can you list five tips of good etiquette for your blog visitors? What about for the blog writer? What five rules of etiquette should *you* follow?

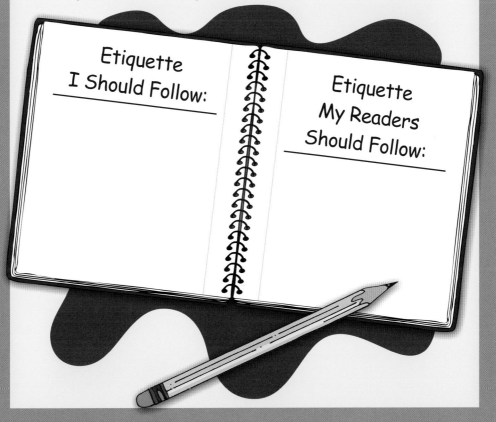

Etiquette
I Should Follow:

Etiquette
My Readers
Should Follow:

CHAPTER FOUR

Online Bullying

Watch out for cyberbullys when you use the Internet.

Bullies pick on people. A bully might push someone down on the playground. He or she might say something mean. That can hurt someone's feelings. But did you know there are bullies on the Internet? A **cyberbully** uses the Internet to pick on others.

Cyberbullies can be just as hurtful as the bullies you meet in person.

How do you know if you are being cyberbullied? You might get **threatening** e-mails from someone you don't know. There might be mean posts on your school online bulletin board. These might say bad things about you.

Cyberbullying is not harmless fun. People who are cyberbullied often become very sad. They may be scared. They may avoid their friends. They may not do their favorite activities.

Remember that good etiquette is also important when you send text messages.

Be careful that you don't cyberbully. Don't send mean e-mails. Don't send threatening text messages. Avoid posting pictures that could embarrass someone. Don't pretend to be someone else. Never trick someone into giving you personal information. Never send someone's personal information to others. Use good online etiquette. Treat others the way you want to be treated.

To get a copy of this activity, visit www.cherrylakepublishing.com/activities.

Activity

Knowing what to do about a cyberbully is important. How much do you know? Below is a list of possible actions. Which actions listed below should you do? Which should you NOT do?

1. Tell a parent, teacher, or trusted adult.
2. Respond to bullying messages.
3. Save bullying messages. Do not delete them.
4. Trust your feelings. If something feels wrong, tell someone.

I am being bullied online.

Answers: 1. yes: always tell an adult as soon as it happens, 2. no: never respond to a cyberbully, 3. yes: saved messages can provide proof of cyberbullying to the police or other authorities, 4. yes: if something feels wrong, it probably is.

Glossary

blog (BLAWG) a Web site that is a personal, online journal with entries from its author

cyberbully (SYE-bur-bu-lee) someone who uses the Internet to threaten, pick on, or spread rumors about others

etiquette (EH-ti-kut) rules for good or polite behavior

online (on-LINE) connected to other computers through the Internet

post (POHST) to put any type of message on a Web site, which includes writing an e-mail

privacy (PRYE-vuh-see) the freedom from having others know or read your thoughts or words

threatening (THREH-ten-ing) mean or scary

Find Out More

BOOKS

Bailey, Diane. *Cyber Ethics*. New York: Rosen Central, 2008.

Jakubiak, David J. *A Smart Kid's Guide to Online Bullying*. New York: PowerKids Press, 2010.

MacEachern, Robyn. *Cyberbullying: Deal with It and Ctrl Alt Delete It*. Toronto, ON: Lorimer, 2011.

WEB SITES

Stop Cyberbullying
www.stopcyberbullying.org/kids/index.html
What is cyberbullying? How does it work? What can you do to prevent it? Check out this site for lots of information about this important subject.

What's the Deal.org
http://deal.org/the-knowzone/internet-safety/
Learn more about Internet etiquette and safety, and about cyberbullying and how to deal with it.

Index

About the Author

Phyllis Cornwall is a media specialist in Michigan. She loves encouraging her students to use online resources in fun, considerate, and safe ways. When not at school, she enjoys spending time with her expanding family.